Phucenschitt

Spirituality For People Who Swear

Lorrie K. Fry

DEDICATION

To all those family, friends, coworkers and brief acquaintances, who have somehow contributed to my spiritual growth. Without those lessons, I would never have needed to follow this path.

Disclaimer:

The information provided in this book is not intended to diagnose, treat or prescribe any condition. One should seek a licensed psychiatrist, counselor, or physician for diagnosis and treatment.

CONTENTS

Introduction:
Spirituality For People Who Swear

Fuck, shit, hell, bitch, asshole, damn, prick. If you are unable to move past those few words, you better box up this book and send it back to Amazon. If you have decided you can handle those words, then you are going to get in-your-face, down-in-the-dirt techniques and guidance to improve your life.

Why am I using swear words in a book about Spirituality? So that people pay attention.

Many people, me included, are annoyed or turned off by organized religion, and therefore, most anything to do with such topics.

Many people, me included, are not, however, turned off by foul language and usually like to swear. So, if you want people

to pay attention, play to their likes.

Do I believe in God? Without a doubt.

And all the names that substitute for the G-

word. I believe in Angels and talk to them

every day. And Fairies. And Aliens. But for

the purposes of this book and to keep an

even playing field, I'm going to refer to God

as "Spirit" and collectively God and all the

rest as "The Universe". Thus, not to offend

anyone. (As though some might not be

offended by the foul language.)

Life can be a raging bitch at times,

but that doesn't mean you need to be one

too. I will teach you how to find your way

back to Spirit and discover your purpose in

life. With a few swear words added in. Just

to keep your attention.

What is spirituality anyway? It is defined in the dictionary as: "of or concerning the spirit".

Hmmm. I think I prefer the description used in a quote by Native American author, Vine Deloria Jr, "Religion is for people who're afraid of going to hell. Spirituality is for those who've already been there."

Some people also believe that Hell is really our human life on Earth.

We come into human existence on Earth primarily to grow our spirit, which grows Spirit, and advances our soul. We agree to forget our connection to Spirit in order to accomplish this. Part of our journey on Earth is to find our way back to Spirit, because if we started already there, what would be the point?

Thus Spirituality.

This book provides steps to find your way back, in a way that you can understand, complete with foul language and song titles. (I'm fucking hammering that shit into your brain, so you damn well remember it.)

Are you paying attention yet?

Part 1
Piece Of My Heart
(Your Birthright)

Let's begin with the basics. It's a

beautiful day. The sun is shining, there are

perfect puffy clouds overhead, you're kicked

back and comfortable, not a worry in the

world. You are in Heaven, after all. And

then you hear The Voice. Spirit is speaking

to you. You sit up and listen, because

everything Spirit tells you is awesome.

"I need you to go and be a human on

Earth," Spirit says.

That's the last thing you expected to

hear. Human. You sigh. You've done that

already, and some of the time it wasn't much

fun. There was pain there and struggle and then death. But this is Spirit talking, so you say "why?"

"I have a task for you, and you are the best qualified."

Oh. Well. You sit up, because to be called "the best qualified" by Spirit is high praise indeed. "What kind of task?" you ask.

"Earth is going through some struggles and I need someone with a big heart who can spread some love and kindness amongst the other humans. Get them back on track and talking to Me again."

Struggles. Fuck. You've been through enough of them. But before you have time to think, your mouth opens and "okay" squeeks out. "Can I pick my family?" you ask.

"Why, of course."

And before you knew it, you were

sliding down some wet, slimy tunnel,

screaming at the top of your lungs, "Wa-a-a-

a-a-it!!!"

"Hi, Baby", you hear a gentle whisper.

You mean I didn't have to go, you think. And

then something sharp pokes you and you

know that Spirit tore out a piece of Its

heart and placed it into the arms of your

human mother. And the journey begins.

By the age of five or so, Spirit begins

to feel like a distant memory. Gone were

the halcyon days of peace and prayer. Gone

were the days of happiness and

contentment. You are about to meet a bully

on the playground and the hell begins.

Time passes. You experience ups and downs, pain, struggle, moments of joy. Your connection to Spirit is as though it never existed. There is an emptiness in your soul that you don't recognize as this loss. You wonder why nothing material really makes you happy except for the fleeting moment of its arrival. Relationships might be good, but some tiny little thing seems disconnected.

Why does your life, even though it's good, feel soooo. . .fucking empty?

And what, or who, is this thing called "Spirit?"

Part 2
Knock, Knock, Knockin' On Heaven's Door
(Connecting With The Universe)

You've begun to crave something

meaningful in your life, but you don't want

some candy-ass spewing sunshine out of his

or her mouth. You want real. You want

something that makes you feel good. You

want. . .well, you don't really know what you want, but it better be something good.

You don't want to spend a bucket of money on it. You don't want more crap to fill your garage. You don't want to listen to some dumb ass spouting rules and nonsense every week. And you aren't about to start wearing robes and draping shit around your neck. Why do you feel this nagging in your soul?

You are craving your connection to

Spirit. You miss that guiding voice talking to

you every day. You miss the wisdom, the

kindness, the "sanity", that is just with you

every day of your life.

What the HELL happened?

First of all, you forgot that you made

that agreement. You were too caught up in

the slimy canal thing to remember that

Spirit said, "find your way back to me!" And now, you are starting to remember.

So how does that happen? It's not like Spirit is, just there, and always available. I mean, you can't see Spirit like before. Maybe Spirit is gone forever. No Way, Jose. Spirit is there for you any time you want. Just knock on the door.

Find yourself a quiet space where you can be alone for a little while. Get comfy; it will help you to remember. Take a few deep breaths and imagine that your heart and mind are opening and becoming aware of what's around you. Think or say out loud "hello, Spirit", and breathe a little more.

Start a dialogue (that means speak out loud) and see what thoughts come into your head. Positive thoughts are Spirit speaking to you. Negative thoughts come

from your Ego, that will try to stop you from

connecting.

When you hear Spirit talking in your

head, you will be filled with a joyous feeling.

Something along the lines of what you get

right after good sex. But better. And not

messy.

Everything in your world will feel right again once you connect with Spirit on a daily – well, sure every minute if you want – basis. Spirit has no sense of time.

The more you connect with Spirit, the better you will begin to feel. You'll start to remember all those things about life and why you are here. You'll remember how to release worry and anxiety. How to ask for help. How to trust that you will be provided for, if you follow your guidance. Life will still have its messy moments, Human, but you will be able to deal with them much easier.

Things and people around you will begin to change as a reflection of who you are becoming. You'll stand up for yourself and stand your ground. You'll be able to speak your truth. People will respect you more. Life will feel more abundant. All because you knocked on the door.

Part 3
Livin' On A Prayer
(The Usefulness Of Prayer)

The P-word. A helluva lot more

frightening than the F-word. You are more

skilled at saying fuck than you are saying

prayer.

Prayer is for. . . nuns or people like that. Heads bowed, on your knees, life of solitude.

It is NOT.

Praying is not just saying a bunch of words someone else wrote up. Praying is just talking to Spirit. Did you know that worry is a form of prayer? Holy Shit! (Yah, it sort of is, isn't it?)

If you can't abide saying the P-word,

come up with something else to call it.

"Talkin' To The Big Cheese." "Dialogue With

The Dude." "Giggles With The Girlfriend."

If you are going to worry about how, then

just start talking to Spirit and ask how to do

it. That's a prayer, tadpole.

Prayer is for you. It is just your

conversation with Spirit about whatever you

want to talk about. Maybe you are in heavy

traffic and some dickhead cut you off.

After you call him an assortment of names,

ask Spirit to bring some measure of serenity

to your drive. Expect it to happen. 'Cause it

will.

I ask Walter The Parking Angel to

help me find a quick, safe spot to park my

beloved Camaro away from the door-dingers.

He is very good at it. Especially when I am

in a hurry.

Prayer helps you keep your sanity during trying days. Prayer helps with pain. Prayer helps your friends when you ask nicely on their behalf. Prayer gets you to say "thank you" when you have had a victorious day.

The most important part of prayer is that it comes from your heart. You gotta feel it to believe it. We tend to pray from the heart when we are in difficult situations.

I know you have been there. I have too.

Down on your knees sobbing with

frustration, your heart ripping in two. That

is praying, my friend.

It doesn't always have to be used

when you are in pain. Why not pray when you

are experiencing joy? Do the Snoopy Dance.

Laugh out loud. "Thank you, thank you, thank

you!" is totally a prayer.

Pray when you can't get past something. It is called a "Change Me" prayer. Change me into someone who can let this go. Change me into someone who can allow good things into my life. Change me into someone who gives a shit. Change me into someone with more patience or whatever.

You get the idea?

Praying is the ticket to a better way

of life. So, get down on your knees. Or not.

The Body
The Energy Never Dies
(Your Energy Body)

You are made up of energy. Little

electromagnetic pulses that circulate in

every single cell of your body. Like fucking

gamma rays, dude! Well, not quite, but you

get the picture. Electromagnetic energy

constantly moves and changes, which means

you can effect change to your cellular structure, or it can be affected by your environment.

If you live in a shitty environment, you can absorb toxic chemicals that can make you sick. You might want to do something about that. Your shitty environment can also include toxic people, which can make you even sicker than breathing air pollution.

Why, because all that negative energy collects in your cellular structure and will make you constantly tired and bitchy and complaining and really no fun to be around. Kind of on your way to asshole status. And you don't have to live like that, so I'm going to teach you a little of that woo-woo voodoo shit to get rid of it.

You, however, are going to have to ditch those toxic friends, coworkers, or partner or it is going to be a constant daily battle just to slide into your happy place.

Now that you know you are made of energy, let's look at that a little closer.

Your body has eight energetic centers [there are more, but we won't go that far] called chakras. Chakra is the Sanskrit word for "wheel", because they are shaped like one. Chakras spin vertically in a vortex, pulling energy into the front of your body and sending it out the back. When they get stuck or dirty you get bitchy, but that can be changed. In the following chapters, we will explore each of those eight chakras and what they do for you.

For now, we will just cover the basics. Imagine a cord running down your body, from the top of your head to the soles of your feet. Attached to the cord are funnel shaped fans, one on the front side of you and one on the back side. The energy comes in through the front and out through the back. You get to decide how fast the fans turn, clockwise or counterclockwise, and if the front and back work in tandem or separately.

I know that is a lot to think about, but once you understand the mechanics they run on their own. You just need to maintain them occasionally.

The speed determines how much energy you need to move through your body. Faster is not necessarily better, if you think of energy as getting shit done.

Clockwise brings the energy in so that is a good thing. Counterclockwise isn't bad, because that is a useful way to unclog yourself. (And no, you won't get diarrhea. Although it can be a by-product of energy detoxification.)

Energy coming in through the front is about receiving and out through the back is giving. You should try to maintain balance in this movement, because too much of either

can be tiring.

For example: your third chakra is the

Solar Plexus and it is situated just slightly

above your navel. It resonates to the color

spectrum frequency of yellow. (Ever hear

the term "yellow-bellied coward"? Now you

know where that came from.) The Solar

Plexus chakra is the seat of your personal

power. Your first thought is "ooh, I want a

lot of that". Not necessarily a good thing, as that might take you into asshole status if you don't practice balance. The energy coming into this area should be of medium intensity and slightly more to the receiving side. If too much goes out, you might be giving away your personal power.

The color of the energy is important too. It should be a pure bright yellow. If it is murky, you could feel or act in a negative manner. A bright sunshine yellow allows you to be assertive and positive at the same time. It is all about having good balance.

Meditation is the best and easiest method to clean up and balance your chakras.

Find a quiet place where you won't be disturbed. Put your cell phone away or turn it off. Don't fret, it will still be there when you are finished. Put the phone down.

Damn it, I told you to put that fucking thing away!!

Make yourself comfortable. It does not matter if you are sitting or lying down. I find that sitting makes it easier to do the visualizations. If you are listening to a

guided meditation, you might fall asleep.

This is not a bad thing. Your brain will still

listen and guide your body through the

steps.

Begin with slow, deep, and even

breaths. "In through nose, out through

mouth, Daniel-san." (The Karate Kid, in case

you forgot.) Deep breathing calms your

heart rate and oxygenates your body. It

also helps you open your heart and mind to hear Spirit as you will often get messages during meditation.

Note here: most people think that you need to completely empty your mind of all thought during meditation. That is not true.

As soon as you begin to relax, all the thoughts of your day with begin to ramble through your brain. That is normal. What you want to do is let go of focusing on any one thought. Just let them ramble around with about as much interest from you as you would watching movie credits scroll up the screen. Unless you are one of the unusual types that like to read the credits, then you need to ignore them.

While the movie credits are scrolling away, imagine there is a giant funnel on the top of your head like the type you use to pour liquid into something. This is all about visualization.

Reach all the way up into the Universe and pull down a brilliant white liquid-like light. You might even see gold sparkles within it. Draw the white light down through the funnel and slowly fill up your body, in reverse, your head down to your toes.

As the white light moves its way downward, feel it push out all the dark, dirty energy out through your feet and into the earth. Don't worry, it won't hurt Mother Earth. She is very skilled at transmuting the negative energy into positive. That's her job, by the way.

Keep doing this until all the yuck is gone.

Hint: you can ask the Universe to make this a continual flow to keep you filled with energy and always connected to It.

Now focus your thoughts to the area at the base of your spine. This is where your Root Chakra is located. See it as a red fan and make it spin clockwise. (When I say "fan", I mean like a cooling fan where the blades turn in a circle.) Red is its energy frequency.

Keep it spinning and move your focus to the pelvic area. This is the Sacral Chakra. Spin it clockwise like the first one. Visualize it as bright orange.

Keep it spinning and move up to the navel area, the location of the Solar Plexus Chakra. See it as a yellow fan and make it spin clockwise. You should feel as though there is a cord of energy connecting the chakras as you slowly move upwards in your

body. They are all energetically connected
and help to keep each other tuned and
supported.

Continue the spinning and move up to
the center of your chest. Here is your
Heart Chakra. Its color is emerald green.
Give it a spin clockwise.

Did you notice that you have a rainbow forming in your body? Your body is like a big crystal radiating a beautiful and powerful rainbow. Cool huh?

Continue to keep all the chakras spinning as you move upwards in your body. Next is the Throat Chakra and its energy is blue.

Moving upwards to the center of your forehead is the Third Eye Chakra. Its energy is indigo, or blue-violet.

Then move up to the crown of your head known as the Crown Chakra. Its energy glows violet.

Finally move up to an area just slightly above your head. This is your Higher Self Chakra. Its color is brilliant white. Your chakras should all be spinning and connected

by an electric cord of either a gold or white

light. Take a moment to visualize this

rainbow of spinning energy inside your body.

See how truly powerful you are? Why would

you even think you have no control over your

life? And they say Unicorns don't exist.

You have now cleansed and balanced your energy system. See how easy that was? Make time to do this each day, if nothing but to give you some peace and quiet for five minutes. If sitting isn't your thing, try a walking meditation. Just don't close your eyes or read text messages while you do it. (I told you to put away your phone! Thought I wouldn't notice, didn't you?)

When you meditate on a regular basis you will find that you feel better, you are less tired, and you are more able to handle stressful situations.

Who doesn't want that?

1st Chakra
Root Down
(The Root Chakra)

The Root Chakra is located at the

base of your spine and it is what grounds you

to the Earth. The energy associated with it

relates to safety, security, money and work.

Think the first level of Maslow's Hierarchy

of Need. It has a corresponding color

vibration of red.

When your Root Chakra is dirty or not spinning, you will exist in a constant state of anxiety. You will fucking freak out if you have a flat tire on the way home from work. You might be on the verge of being homeless. Money slides through your fingers like Jello. You might be scared, broke and alone. Can it get any goddamn worse?

Possibly. But you can change it.

There is a whole aspect to changing your belief system in order to change your life, but that is beyond the scope of this book. If you have serious issues, beyond those I've mentioned such as mental health or substance abuse, get thee to a medical or psychological professional and get back on track. There is too much living to be done and you ought not to be suffering in silence.

I mean that. Do not suffer alone. Do not be miserable. There are people who can and will help you.

If your life is reasonably stable and you have housing, food, a job, enough cash to live on, but you have a bit of a roller coaster ride, it could be just toxic energy. Use the meditation technique to clear it out.

Look at your environment. Do you have friends or acquaintances that ask for money or expect you to support them? Practice saying no. And then tell them no. If you must, in order to get the message through their head, tell them "Fucking no and I'm not telling you again!". Your friends are capable of working, finding housing and supporting themselves. You are not their keeper. It is one thing to be generous and charitable and another to be bled dry.

What about your job? Do you like

what you do? Are you good at it? Or are

you better than it and underemployed? How

can you make changes to help you to find

something that will serve you more? Notice,

I said "serve you". Yes, you work in

exchange for a paycheck, but you should

derive some sense of satisfaction from what

you do.

What about your housing? Are you content with your surroundings or are you married to a mortgage? When housing costs are high, it can be difficult to handle rent or a mortgage. Research your area and look at your options. Just don't take to the streets. The energy there will sap the life out of you and keep you stuck in a place of fear and lack. Rent out a friend's basement. You'll have a safe place to live and they'll have help with the rent or mortgage.

Everything begins with a foundation

and that foundation needs to be a strong one

to support all that you are building upon it.

Such as your life.

Now send that Root deep down into

Mother Earth and draw the energy upwards.

If She can grow a tree, why can't it be you?

2nd Chakra
Sooner Or Later You're Addicted
(The Sacral Chakra)

The Sacral Chakra is in the pelvic area

in front of your sacrum and it is connected

to your emotional body. The energy

associated with it relates to pleasure. Why

do you think it is located where it is?

Pleasure is all about how you feel. Feelings

help you to connect to others and have

relationships. When you don't acknowledge

and allow your feelings to be expressed,

what do you think happens?

Addictions, my friend.

Things that you think make you feel

good, but only just cover up what really

makes you feel good. It starts by being

honest with yourself. Yes, maybe you've

experienced pain and heartbreak in your life.

Maybe you stuffed those feelings down

because they are too overwhelming to deal

with. Well, you know what? Your body

knows how to deal with them.

Shaking, crying, howling gets the

crappy feelings and stress out of your body.

And don't worry, you won't cry endlessly,

your body knows when to stop. And when

you stop, you will feel better with a deep

sense of relief. After that, you can get in

touch with your real feelings and you won't

need food or alcohol or drugs or anything

else to make yourself feel good.

Allowing yourself to have feelings

opens doors to parts of yourself you might

not know are there, such as creativity and

great ideas.

The sacral chakra totally rules amazing ideas.

The flip side of pleasure is creativity. Think about another word for sex: procreate. Pro-create. Haven't you ever wondered what color to paint the kitchen when you are having sex? You haven't? You lie like a rug. Okay, all kidding aside, good feelings open pathways in the brain. You are relaxed and happy, and that is when you are most able to hear Spirit's suggestions for you. A great presentation, a beautiful garment, spectacular painting, or a killer book proposal.

And just a little tidbit: when your Sacral and Throat chakras are functioning at optimal levels, you will be able to share your ideas with others. Cha-ching!

3rd Chakra
It's My Life
(The Solar Plexus Chakra)

The Solar Plexus Chakra is located

right below your navel and it is connected to

your personal power. The energy associated

with it determines how you exercise control

and create self-boundaries.

There is an old expression "venting your spleen". Sounds a little gross, but it relates to speaking out on behalf of yourself. Not being a doormat.

Personal power can wear many faces. A yellow smiley face says I'm happy, I have good boundaries and I am not afraid to speak my truth in a positively assertive way. A dirty yellow frowny face says I am a doormat, my needs are never honored, and I complain about it incessantly.

It can also be the dark, menacing face of a bully.

It takes practice to have balanced personal power. You must first learn to honor your needs yourself and not expect others to do it for you. When you are tired, say so and go to bed. Don't wait until you are bitchy and blurry-eyed and someone says, "will you go lie down?!" Practicing good self-care is the first step in creating effective personal power.

The second step is saying "no" to unreasonable demands of your time. Your teenager is capable of making a sandwich. Your coworker can type just as fast as you. And you don't need to give money to the solicitor at your door if you don't believe in

the charity that they are selling. "No" is a

complete sentence.

It might not be easy to say it the

first few times around, especially if you are

the kind, giving type. But an exhausted,

broke you is not going to feel like

communicating with Spirit, whose help you so

desperately need.

Lack of personal power keeps you in a state of fear. Anxiety will rule your body and your mind will make up all sorts of shit that may or may not happen. Tune up your chakra and clear the fear.

4th Chakra
Love Is All Around Us
(The Heart Chakra)

The Heart Chakra is located right in

the center of your chest and it is connected

to your ability to give and receive love. The

energy associated with it is obviously love.

It starts with self-love. Do you love yourself? No? Why not? Spirit loves you and thinks you are awesome. (Remember, you were chosen by Spirit to help heal the Earth through love.)

If you do love yourself, then teach others how to do the same. Most people don't really love themselves, you know. In essence, it is probably true since we incarnate as humans to learn how.

When you love yourself first, you are able to open your heart to give and receive love from others. You are able to weather heartbreak and allow yourself to experience love in all its forms.

Puppies love you, right? They do it with pure, unconditional love. Same as babies and kittens and rhinoceros. Yes, they do, I saw it on You Tube. House cats, maybe not so much. But I'm getting off track here.

Not loving yourself can create a

multitude of health issues. Sure, each

chakra represents specific areas of the

body, but your heart rules all. It carries

blood to every inch of you so you want the

quality of that blood to be optimal, and

strangely enough your thoughts can create

disease.

The Heart Chakra is located between

of all the chakras. It connects the lower

three, earth-based with the upper three,

spirit-based so that we may experience our

humanness fully complete. The Heart

connects everything. The energy of the

heart is Love and it is the most powerful

energy of all. When you can stay focused in

love, nothing can truly harm you. Sure,

someone could cut off your hand and that

would harm you. But if you can hold the

energy of love in your heart, you will still

love yourself and still be capable even

without one hand.

Don't have a partner, but want one?

Treat yourself as you want to be treated.

You'll put that energy out there and attract

the right one. Like attracts like, after all.

Now go stand in front of a mirror and say, "I Love You". Yes, you can do it. Even without your cell phone.

5th Chakra
Tell It Like It Is
(The Throat Chakra)

The Throat Chakra is located right at

the base of your throat and it is connected

to your ability to speak your truth. The

energy associated with it is communication

and expression.

Got thyroid problems? They are energetically related to not being able to speak your needs. Do you constantly clear your throat? If so, what are you holding back? Speaking your truth does not mean it will come out ugly and demanding. Honesty in your feelings can be very loving. Ask the Universe for help with the words.

Many people resort to technology to communicate. Technology gives us the ability to reach out globally for business, support, ideas and new friendships. Just don't let it replace good old eye contact. It is far easier to type "fuck you" than say it to someone's face. And Unfriending someone? Seriously?! That's like being in Junior High and delivering notes on someone else's behalf. Don't act like a jerk. You'll just clog up your throat chakra and you won't be able to eat cheeseburgers anymore.

Use meditation to get the energy unstuck. Rehearse important speeches in front of a mirror so you can monitor your body language and watch the movement of your mouth. People will get what you are saying when they see it in your eyes. Especially when you say, "I love you".

They will likely follow that with a hug, and you'll get a free tune-up of your heart chakra as a bonus.

Say what you mean and mean what you say.

6th Chakra
I Can See Clearly Now
(The Third Eye Chakra)

The Third Eye Chakra is located right

in the middle of your forehead and it is

connected to your ability to see beyond the

senses. The energy associated with it is

intuition and empathy.

Ever have those moments when you get that "wonky" feeling that something isn't right? Or you are around someone that you don't like and don't know the reason? You might even have a squirrely feeling in your gut. That is your intuition kicking in.

Everyone has the innate ability to be intuitive; we just don't always use it. Or maybe don't want to. I call it the "Inner Bullshit Detector". Use it. It is there to

protect you in not-so-good situations. It is
also an open channel to receive awesome
ideas, just like I'm doing now.

When you really open your third eye
chakra, life will go smoother. Opening it is
easy, just imagine there is a window shade in
your forehead and you just push it up with
your finger. Any finger will do, even THAT
one. It is much easier to do during a
meditation session, because you are relaxed.

Getting it to open and staying that way might take numerous attempts, depending on your belief system. Eventually you will see an eyeball looking back at you. It's yours, silly, but don't be surprised if it is a different color. Mine is a sparkly emerald green even though I have brown eyes, thereby proving that I am not full of shit.

When I am searching for insight into a situation, I'll briefly close my eyes and "look through" the eyeball. Messages or visions will come into my head. Spirit is coming through loud and clear. If you get a bit of a headache, just ask that the energy slows down. You will eventually work up to an ever-higher energy and you will see even more.

Advanced skill in this area is clairvoyance, the ability to see energy. Yes, that means psychic. Like anything else, it takes practice and developing trust in the messages or visions you are receiving from the Universe. Universe equals positive messages and continual nudging. Ego equals negative messages and OMG, I gotta do this NOW! Being psychic is very useful and you are not whacked out. I've been doing this a long time and have been a big help to friends. Clearly you can see (ahem) how

useful this can be for you so work on opening

that Cyclops eyeball. No one can see it but

you.

7th Chakra
Hold Your Head High
(The Crown Chakra)

The Crown Chakra is located at the

crown of your head and it is connected to

consciousness, spirituality and the Universe.

The energy associated with it is

transcendence and helps move the energy

into the lower chakras.

It is also related to the pituitary gland and helps facilitate the activities of the endocrine system. Because it is located at the crown of your head it also stimulates the brain and nervous system, which is why you can use meditation to attain a state of relaxation. Now do you understand why meditation is so important for your health? It doesn't cost a cent and you won't stink up the house like skunk. (I think you know what I am referring to.)

This is your link to returning to the Universe. A blocked crown chakra will have you feeling empty and as though there is no purpose to your life. This chakra is the most difficult one to keep clean, because of our belief systems.

When you doubt yourself, this chakra is blocked and dirty. When your life feels hopeless or meaningless, it is blocked and dirty. For many people, unblocking it is fearful.

Do not fear this. Everything you need comes down through your crown chakra. Your connection to the Universe is what you are striving for in human life. Your path back, and I'm not talking death, is through your crown chakra. Clean it the fuck up!

It will feel like a beanie cap is sitting on the back of your head. Reach up there and energetically yank that fugly thing off. No, your brain won't ooze out of your head nor will it suddenly be filled with a bunch of voices. What you might feel is a sense of peace, of rightness, of knowing that things are better.

Imagine there is a funnel on your head. Seriously. It won't mess up your hair and no one will see it. Except maybe psychic people and that's okay. They will stare just above your head, mumbling "I see." Not really.

Let the brilliant white light energy of the Universe pour into the funnel. No, it won't make you sick like too much vodka. However, you might feel a little giddy at first just because it feels so good. Go ahead, do a little dance, no one is watching. Think of how good you will feel if you keep this funnel filled. Don't worry about anything bad coming in. The funnel is only open to the Universe.

Always keep that funnel open to the Universe, then your life will have meaning and you will feel like holding your head high.

8th Chakra
Bring Me A Higher Love
(The Higher Self Chakra)

The Higher Self Chakra is located

approximately two feet above your head, and

it connects you to greater realms of the

Universe. The energy associated with it is

knowingness, divine love and spiritual

compassion.

This chakra connects your physical body with your soul. You can access divine parts of yourself, connect with higher spiritual beings, advance your spiritual gifts and clear karmic residue. You can connect to the Higher Self during meditation. Do I need to remind you how important meditation is for you?

Your Higher Self always knows that shit's going to turn out okay. Your Higher Self has access to Divine information and spirit guides so why wouldn't you listen to it instead of some dumb fuck on the radio?

But in order to experience human life you need to be just a little bit of a dumb fuck yourself. See if we already knew everything, and did everything the best or right way, then there would be nothing left

to learn.

We are still in Junior High, sending

stupid texts and laughing about farts.

You could access your Higher Self all

the time to make your life easier. It won't

be perfection because that is not possible.

But what if your coworker is acting like a

jerk and dumping all their work on you, and

your boss won't listen to your complaints because the jerk is a boy genius. Connect with your Higher Self for some guidance. Visualize a prayer going straight up into a glowing ball above your head. Just ask for help, but nothing specific. Expect that the answer is in that ball and you have access to it. Don't put a time frame or any other expectation on that answer.

Then don't be surprised if the next day Boy Genius tells you he has a fabulous job offer from another company and will likely be leaving in two weeks, because if the Universe wants something out of your life it will happen. However, sometimes we need "difficult" situations in our life. They help us grow and usually force us to make changes that are ultimately for our highest good. Connecting with your Higher Self can help make that transition a little less painful and help you see the good in it.

Your Higher Self is connected to all

the spiritual beings. Archangels, angels,

guardian angels, spirit guides, spiritual

teachers, dearly departed, elementals

(Fairies and the like) and so on. Now I'm

talking good spiritual beings, no evil shit

here. Evil shit is only your Ego making you

think they exist. Except for Aliens. That

shit is real. So, if someone is looking at you

with what appears - just briefly - like

stainless steel eyes, get the hell away from

them. They stick on you like leeches and

suck all the energy out of you. They might

even make you sick.

This chakra will help you clear out

your old karmic residue. These are behavior

patterns that you bring into your life to heal

and balance. Been doing the same shit, over

and over, for too long? I'm not necessarily

talking about doing work, although that is an

aspect. Karma usually revolves around

relationships. Being a victim, for example.

You will keep getting yourself involved with

people who harm you in some way, doesn't

have to be just physical. Maybe you keep

asking yourself, "why do I let that happen?".

That is a nudge from the Universe that it is

time to clean that shit up. It may involve

therapy or healers or some such, but it

definitely means changing your behavior.

(Your Throat Chakra might also need some cleanup work so you can say "no" more frequently.)

Ask your Spirit Guides or Guardian Angels to help you. That is what they are there for. The memory of the pattern might remain, but the behavior will change. Who knows, your head might feel lighter and you won't have a neck ache anymore.

Your Soul will thank you and Spirit will benefit from your growth.

Final Notes
Losing My Religion

I was raised in a religion-oriented household. We went to services each week, gave money, followed the rules (mostly), and accepted the idea that we would go straight to Hell for any perceived transgression. Eating meat on Friday would have you going straight to Hell. But hey, barbecue, right?

The doctrine was based upon an enormous amount of guilt, yet punishment was meted out with endless praying. So why not just pray a bunch all the time so you would be forgiven before you sinned?

I'm certain it was not viewed that way.

I'm certain of a lot of things about religion and most of it is centered around not talking to [God or insert name] Spirit. I asked that once-upon-a-time: "why can't I talk directly to God?". Questions like that are not appreciated, and then you get more rules to follow.

I dutifully went to religious education, which was more about the doctrine than about God or any other spiritual being. It all seemed silly to me so when I was about 15 years of age, I went to the local library for some education. Our local librarian was

quite liberal in his beliefs, so the library was

filled with many books on many subjects,

including the topic of spirituality.

I spent days in and out of the stacks,

reading about all the different world

religions. When I finished them, I moved on

to pagan studies, Wicca, Shamans and the

like. Then onto metaphysics, which became

my lifetime interest.

Do you know what I learned?

Each one is based upon a series of rules, written by (mostly) men in silly clothes, that dictate how, when and where to worship and exactly what to believe, but really had little to do with a non-human supreme being.

Where was Spirit in all this? And why couldn't I speak directly to It? It was then that I lost my religion.

Suddenly, meaning in my life took on a whole new "meaning". No more stupid rules, no worries about beef or pork, no middleman to play "telephone" on my behalf.

Anytime, anywhere, any place, I could speak to Spirit. And Spirit spoke back.

Ignorance breeds fear or so I say.

No worries about what someone else might

believe. Acceptance that they are doing

what is best for them. Other than I do not

condone harming or killing in the name of

your belief. Spirit does not want that

either. Spirit is all about L.O.V.E. – Learning

Our Very Existence. I just made that up,

but it makes sense.

What is the definition of religion?

According to the online Merriam

Webster it says:

1a: the state of a religious

a nun in her 20th year of religion

b (1): the service and worship of God

or the supernatural

(2): commitment or devotion to

religious faith or observance

2: a personal set or institutionalized

system of religious attitudes, beliefs,

and practices

3 archaic: scrupulous conformity:

conscientiousness

4: a cause, principle, or system of

beliefs held to with ardor and faith

That might be the definition given by

M.W., but the whole thing is pretty much

fucked-up. I think b (1) is mostly forgotten

and #4 explains the current state of

nuttiness.

So much for keeping God in the right place.

These are my opinions, after all. Not all of it is a mess. Some people really do walk their talk and connect with Spirit.

Gathering together in a beautiful building to share your beliefs just makes them stronger.

All that positive energy is very powerful too. Many people like rituals. I like some too, just not the ones that take me away from talking to Spirit. Because if someone tells you that is not allowed, then you better be losing your religion.

In The End

So, what have we learned here? Our existence is created because Spirit asked us to come to Earth to learn about being human, to love and be loved, and to find our way back to Spirit armed with a whole lot of experience. That wouldn't be so bad if it weren't for all the extra shit we had to go through.

To compensate for that, Spirit filled us with a longing for something that inspired us to get through the shitty times. A sort of emptiness that made us just know there was something more. So, one day we just said, "are You out there?" and we began to remember where we came from.

We learned how to pray in words that made sense to us even if no one else understood or liked what we said. But the prayers worked and sometimes made miracles out of the shit pile.

We discovered that our bodies are more than just flesh, blood, bones and stuff. That we could, in effect, change our cellular structure and our belief system by visualizing something different. We learned how to keep our energetic body in tune so it would perform optimally.

From there we discovered that it was possible to connect directly to Spirit and all the other spiritual beings available to assist us.

We decided that religion had its place in our life, but only if it supported our connection to Spirit.

So now what?

If you are reading this, then the journey is not finished. It never will be as our Soul is eternal even if our physical bodies are not. You are on a journey, Young Skywalker, that can bring you peace, bliss, love and a whole hell lot of fun. Feel the Force, baby!

Fuck, yeah!

ABOUT THE AUTHOR

Lorrie has studied, researched and practiced metaphysical and spiritual concepts since she was fifteen years of age. She developed her skills of clairvoyance and clairaudience, mostly to use them in daily life, but for providing insight and guidance to others. Personal difficulties inspired her to research self-help and incorporate those techniques for a better life. Lorrie is an urban dweller in Denver, Colorado. For more profound and profane guidance, you can find her on her blog: www.lovingyoursh-t.com